This Journal Belongs to:

_____

Letter of Affirmation

(Look in the mirror. Read it. Recite it. Read it again and then memorize it.)

Today I choose me. Within these pages are my dreams, my goals, my fears, my wins and my lessons. It is through these pages that I explore the depths of my being, the complexity and simplicity of my life. I am growing. I am learning more and more about who I am. I am worthy as is, without change. I am multi-dimensional and learning daily to love every part of me, through every season. I am using journaling to engage in self-care and to chronicle this voyage we call life. The journey continues...

The Self-Care Advocate

Today's Date : _ _ _ _ _ _ _ _ _ _

List 3 things you are grateful for:

1. ....

2. ....

3. ....

What does self-care mean to you?

_____

_____

_____

_____

_____

_____

_____

_____

_____

_____

_____

_____

_____

_____

_____

_____

"You are worth the investment you make to
help you grow to your fullest potential."

– Ayana Shepherd, MSW

Today's Date : _ _ _ _ _ _ _ _ _ _

Today's Date : _ _ _ _ _ _ _ _ _ _ _

Today's Date : _ _ _ _ _ _ _ _ _ _ _

List 3 things you are grateful for:

1. ....

2. ....

3. ....

How are you feeling today?
Describe with words or by drawing your feelings.

"Almost everything will work again if you
unplug it."

— Anne Lamott

Today's Date : _____

Today's Date : _____

Today's Date : _ _ _ _ _ _ _ _ _ _

List 3 things you are grateful for:

1. ....

2. ....

3. ....

Name a song that makes you feel good. Why?

_____

_____

_____

_____

_____

_____

_____

_____

_____

_____

_____

_____

_____

_____

"Breathe. Let go. Remember, this is the only
moment you have for sure."

– Oprah Winfrey

Today's Date : _ _ _ _ _ _ _ _ _ _

Today's Date : _ _ _ _ _ _ _ _ _ _ _

Today's Date : _ _ _ _ _ _ _ _ _ _ _

List 3 things you are grateful for:

1.

2.

3.

What is something you want to accomplish in the next month? Year? 5 Years?

_____

_____

_____

_____

_____

_____

_____

_____

_____

_____

_____

_____

_____

"You're braver than you believe, and stronger than you
seem, and smarter than you think."

- A.A. Mine

Today's Date : _____

Today's Date : _ _ _ _ _ _ _ _ _ _ _

Today's Date : _ _ _ _ _ _ _ _ _ _

List 3 things you are grateful for:

1.
2.
3.

What is one thing you can do today to work toward your goals?

"It always seems impossible until it is done."

- Nelson Mandela

Today's Date : _____

Today's Date : _____

Today's Date : _ _ _ _ _ _ _ _ _ _ _

List 3 things you are grateful for:

1. ....
2. ....
3. ....

What are five things you love about yourself?

_____

_____

_____

_____

_____

_____

_____

_____

_____

_____

_____

_____

_____

_____

_____

_____

"The challenge is not to be perfect; it is to be whole."

— Jane Fonda

Today's Date : _____

Today's Date : _ _ _ _ _ _ _ _ _ _

Today's Date : _ _ _ _ _ _ _ _ _ _

List 3 things you are grateful for:

1. ....

2. ....

3. ....

What are some things you do when you are feeling down?

_____

_____

_____

_____

_____

_____

_____

_____

_____

_____

_____

_____

_____

"As you grow older you will discover that you have two
hands, one for helping yourself, the
other for helping others."

-Maya Angelou

Today's Date : _____

Today's Date : _____

Today's Date : _ _ _ _ _ _ _ _ _ _ _

List 3 things you are grateful for:

1.

2.

3.

What are things you do to improve your mood?

"Talk to yourself like you would to someone
you love."

— Brene Brown

Today's Date : _____

Today's Date : _ _ _ _ _ _ _ _ _ _ _

Today's Date : _ _ _ _ _ _ _ _ _ _

List 3 things you are grateful for:

1.

2.

3.

What does your morning routine look like?
What can be added to your routine?

"You can't pour from an empty cup."

– Author Unknown

Today's Date : _____

Today's Date : _____

Today's Date : _ _ _ _ _ _ _ _ _ _ _

List 3 things you are grateful for:

1. ....

2. ....

3. ....

Write about when you overcame an obstacle.

_____

_____

_____

_____

_____

_____

_____

_____

_____

_____

_____

_____

_____

_____

_____

_____

"The only time you fail is when you fall down and stay down."

- Stephen Richards

Today's Date : _____

Today's Date : _____

Today's Date : _ _ _ _ _ _ _ _ _ _

List 3 things you are grateful for:

1. ....

2. ....

3. ....

What gets in the way of you engaging in self-care?

_____

_____

_____

_____

_____

_____

_____

_____

_____

_____

_____

_____

_____

_____

"Self-care is a lifestyle."

- Ayana Shepherd, MSW

Today's Date : _ _ _ _ _ _ _ _ _ _ _

Today's Date : _ _ _ _ _ _ _ _ _ _ _

Today's Date : _ _ _ _ _ _ _ _ _ _ _

List 3 things you are grateful for:

1. ....

2. ....

3. ....

Write about your day.

_____

_____

_____

_____

_____

_____

_____

_____

_____

_____

_____

_____

_____

_____

"Every day may not be good... but there is good in every day."

- Alice Morse Earle

Today's Date : _____

Today's Date : _____

Today's Date : _ _ _ _ _ _ _ _ _ _

List 3 things you are grateful for:

1. ....

2. ....

3. ....

List your coping skills and when they work best.

_____

_____

_____

_____

_____

_____

_____

_____

_____

_____

_____

_____

_____

_____

"Keep your head up."

– Tupac Shakur

Today's Date : _ _ _ _ _ _ _ _ _ _

Today's Date : _____

Today's Date : _ _ _ _ _ _ _ _ _ _

List 3 things you are grateful for:

1.

2.

3.

Write in detail about what made you happy today.

"The best thing you can do for a person is to inspire them."

– Nipsey Hussle

Today's Date : _____

Today's Date : _ _ _ _ _ _ _ _ _ _ _

Today's Date : _ _ _ _ _ _ _ _ _ _

List 3 things you are grateful for:

1. ....

2. ....

3. ....

Write about what causes you stress and why? How do you react?
What can you do differently?

_____

_____

_____

_____

_____

_____

_____

_____

_____

_____

_____

_____

_____

_____

"Breathe in, breathe out."

- Kanye West

Today's Date : _ _ _ _ _ _ _ _ _ _

Today's Date : _____

Today's Date : _ _ _ _ _ _ _ _ _ _ _

List 3 things you are grateful for:

1. ....

2. ....

3. ....

How do you know you are feeling anxious?
How do you regulate your anxiety?

_____

_____

_____

_____

_____

_____

_____

_____

_____

_____

_____

_____

_____

"Almost everything will work again if you
unplug it."

— Anne Lamott

Today's Date : _ _ _ _ _ _ _ _ _ _

Today's Date : _____

Today's Date : _ _ _ _ _ _ _ _ _ _

List 3 things you are grateful for:

1. ....
2. ....
3. ....

What are some things on your bucket list?

_____

_____

_____

_____

_____

_____

_____

_____

_____

_____

_____

_____

_____

_____

_____

_____

"Breathe. Let go. Remember, this is the only
moment you have for sure."

– Oprah Winfrey

Today's Date : _____

Today's Date : _____

Today's Date : _ _ _ _ _ _ _ _ _ _ _

List 3 things you are grateful for:

1. ....

2. ....

3. ....

How do you feel about exercise?

_____

_____

_____

_____

_____

_____

_____

_____

_____

_____

_____

_____

_____

_____

_____

"Progress over perfection."

– David Perlmutter

Today's Date : _ _ _ _ _ _ _ _ _ _

Today's Date : _ _ _ _ _ _ _ _ _ _

Today's Date : _____

List 3 things you are grateful for:

1. ....
2. ....
3. ....

Do you struggle with telling people "No"? Why?

_____

_____

_____

_____

_____

_____

_____

_____

_____

_____

_____

_____

_____

_____

_____

"Your power lies in setting boundaries."

- Ayana Shepherd, MSW

Today's Date : _ _ _ _ _ _ _ _ _ _ _

Today's Date : _____

Today's Date : _____

List 3 things you are grateful for:

1. ....

2. ....

3. ....

What are ways that you set healthy boundaries
with friends or family?

_____

_____

_____

_____

_____

_____

_____

_____

_____

_____

_____

_____

_____

_____

_____

"The challenge is not to be perfect; it is to be
whole."

– Jane Fonda

Today's Date : _ _ _ _ _ _ _ _ _ _ _

Today's Date : _____

Today's Date : _ _ _ _ _ _ _ _ _ _ _

List 3 things you are grateful for:

1. ....

2. ....

3. ....

Who is a part of your support system/circle of support? Why?

_____

_____

_____

_____

_____

_____

_____

_____

_____

_____

_____

_____

_____

_____

"As you grow older you will discover that you have two
hands, one for helping yourself, the
other for helping others."

-Maya Angelou

Today's Date : _ _ _ _ _ _ _ _ _ _ _

Today's Date : _ _ _ _ _ _ _ _ _ _ _

Today's Date : _____

List 3 things you are grateful for:

1. ....

2. ....

3. ....

What is something you wish people knew about you?

_____

_____

_____

_____

_____

_____

_____

_____

_____

_____

_____

_____

_____

_____

_____

"Talk to yourself like you would to someone
you love."

— Brene Brown

Today's Date : _____

Today's Date : _ _ _ _ _ _ _ _ _ _

Today's Date : _____

1. _____

2. _____

3. _____

What was one of the most difficult things you had to endure?
What did you learn from the experience?

_____

_____

_____

_____

_____

_____

_____

_____

_____

_____

_____

_____

_____

_____

_____

"When life serves you lemons, make
lemonade."

- Dale Carnegie

Today's Date : _ _ _ _ _ _ _ _ _ _

Today's Date : _____

Today's Date : _____

List 3 things you are grateful for:

1. ....

2. ....

3. ....

If you could go anywhere in the world with no limitations
where would you go?
Who would you take with you?
What would you do once you get there?

_____

_____

_____

_____

_____

_____

_____

_____

_____

_____

_____

_____

_____

_____

"Life is a journey, not a destination."

- Ralph Waldo Emerson

Today's Date : _____

Today's Date : _ _ _ _ _ _ _ _ _ _ _

Today's Date : _____

1.

2.

3.

If money wasn't a concern what would your dream job be?
Why?

"Twenty years from now you will be more disappointed by the things that you didn't do than by the ones you did do."

- H. Jackson Brown, Jr.

Today's Date : _ _ _ _ _ _ _ _ _ _

Today's Date : _____

Today's Date : _ _ _ _ _ _ _ _ _ _

List 3 things you are grateful for:

1. ....

2. ....

3. ....

What boundaries can you set in order to support your own
mental and physical wellness?
What steps will you take to set those boundaries?

_____

_____

_____

_____

_____

_____

_____

_____

_____

_____

_____

_____

_____

_____

"We cannot direct the wind, but we can adjust the sails."

– Dolly Parton

Today's Date : ＿＿＿＿＿＿＿＿＿＿＿

Today's Date : _ _ _ _ _ _ _ _ _ _

Today's Date : _ _ _ _ _ _ _ _ _ _ _

List 3 things you are grateful for:

1. ....

2. ....

3. ....

What do you look for in a friend? Of those qualities which do you
possess? How can you be a better friend?

_____

_____

_____

_____

_____

_____

_____

_____

_____

_____

_____

_____

_____

"Courage is going after what you want even when you are
afraid. Do it anyway."

— Ayana Shepherd, MSW

Today's Date : _ _ _ _ _ _ _ _ _ _ _

Today's Date : _____

Today's Date : _ _ _ _ _ _ _ _ _ _ _

List 3 things you are grateful for:

1. ....

2. ....

3. ....

If you could go back in time and give the younger you advice,
what would you tell yourself?

_____

_____

_____

_____

_____

_____

_____

_____

_____

_____

_____

_____

_____

_____

_____

"Progress over perfection."

– David Perlmutter

Today's Date : _ _ _ _ _ _ _ _ _ _

Today's Date : _____

Today's Date : _ _ _ _ _ _ _ _ _ _ _

List 3 things you are grateful for:

1. ....

2. ....

3. ....

Name and describe your safe space.

_____

_____

_____

_____

_____

_____

_____

_____

_____

_____

_____

_____

_____

_____

_____

_____

"Beauty begins the moment you decide to be
yourself."

– Coco Chanel

Today's Date : _ _ _ _ _ _ _ _ _ _ _

Today's Date : _ _ _ _ _ _ _ _ _ _

Today's Date : _ _ _ _ _ _ _ _ _ _ _

List 3 things you are grateful for:

1. ....

2. ....

3. ....

What self-care activities do you enjoy most?
Are there others you'd like to increase? Why?

_____

_____

_____

_____

_____

_____

_____

_____

_____

_____

_____

_____

_____

"Self-care is a necessity, not a luxury!"

- Author Unknown

Today's Date : _____

Today's Date : _____

Today's Date : _____

| List 3 things you are grateful for: |

1. ....

2. ....

3. ....

How do you show yourself kindness, compassion and grace, daily?

_____

_____

_____

_____

_____

_____

_____

_____

_____

_____

_____

_____

_____

_____

_____

_____

"I am fearfully and wonderfully made."

– Psalms 139:14

Today's Date : _____

Today's Date : _____

Today's Date : _____

List 3 things you are grateful for:

1. ....
2. ....
3. ....

What are some of your favorite hobbies?
When was the last time you engaged in that hobby?
How can you incorporate the hobby into your life more?

_____

_____

_____

_____

_____

_____

_____

_____

_____

_____

_____

_____

_____

_____

"We cannot direct the wind, but we can adjust the sails."

– Dolly Parton

Today's Date : _____

Today's Date : _____

Today's Date : _____

1. ....
2. ....
3. ....

If you were to be an animal, what animal would you choose to be?
Why?

_____

_____

_____

_____

_____

_____

_____

_____

_____

_____

_____

_____

_____

_____

"Don't just follow the herd. Be like a bird. Open your wings
and fly high in the sky!"

- Author Unknown

Today's Date : _ _ _ _ _ _ _ _ _ _

Today's Date : _ _ _ _ _ _ _ _ _ _

Today's Date : _ _ _ _ _ _ _ _ _ _

List 3 things you are grateful for:

1. ....

2. ....

3. ....

List some of your favorites: books, songs, food items, movies, places you've visited, scents, people you admire etc.

_____

_____

_____

_____

_____

_____

_____

_____

_____

_____

_____

_____

_____

"Self-Care is a Lifestyle."

- Ayana Shepherd, MSW

Today's Date : _ _ _ _ _ _ _ _ _ _ _

Today's Date : _ _ _ _ _ _ _ _ _ _ _

Today's Date : _ _ _ _ _ _ _ _ _ _ _

List 3 things you are grateful for:

1.

2.

3.

List 10 things or people that motivate or inspire you.

"The best thing you can do for a person is to
inspire them."

- Nipsey Hussle

Today's Date : _ _ _ _ _ _ _ _ _ _

Today's Date : _ _ _ _ _ _ _ _ _ _

Today's Date : _ _ _ _ _ _ _ _ _ _

List 3 things you are grateful for:

1.
2.
3.

What do you look forward to most in the future?

_____

_____

_____

_____

_____

_____

_____

_____

_____

_____

_____

_____

_____

_____

_____

_____

"You are worth the investment you make to
help you grow to your fullest potential."

– Ayana Shepherd, MSW

Today's Date : _ _ _ _ _ _ _ _ _ _

Today's Date : _ _ _ _ _ _ _ _ _ _

Today's Date : _ _ _ _ _ _ _ _ _ _ _

List 3 things you are grateful for:

1. ....

2. ....

3. ....

What are 3 things you can't live without? Why?

_____

_____

_____

_____

_____

_____

_____

_____

_____

_____

_____

_____

_____

_____

_____

"Keep your head up."

– Tupac Shakur

Today's Date : _ _ _ _ _ _ _ _ _ _

Today's Date : _ _ _ _ _ _ _ _ _ _

Today's Date : ＿＿＿＿＿＿＿＿＿＿＿

Today's Date : _ _ _ _ _ _ _ _ _ _ _

Today's Date : _ _ _ _ _ _ _ _ _ _

Today's Date : _ _ _ _ _ _ _ _ _ _

Today's Date : _ _ _ _ _ _ _ _ _ _ _

Today's Date : _ _ _ _ _ _ _ _ _ _

Today's Date : _ _ _ _ _ _ _ _ _ _

Today's Date : _ _ _ _ _ _ _ _ _ _

Today's Date : _ _ _ _ _ _ _ _ _ _

Today's Date : _ _ _ _ _ _ _ _ _ _

Today's Date : _____

Today's Date : _____

Today's Date : _ _ _ _ _ _ _ _ _ _

Today's Date : _ _ _ _ _ _ _ _ _ _

Today's Date : _ _ _ _ _ _ _ _ _ _ _

Today's Date : _ _ _ _ _ _ _ _ _ _

Today's Date : _ _ _ _ _ _ _ _ _ _ _

Today's Date : _ _ _ _ _ _ _ _ _ _

Today's Date : _ _ _ _ _ _ _ _ _ _ _

Today's Date : _ _ _ _ _ _ _ _ _ _

Today's Date : _ _ _ _ _ _ _ _ _ _

Today's Date : _____

Today's Date : _____

Today's Date : _ _ _ _ _ _ _ _ _ _

Today's Date : _____

Today's Date : _____

Made in the USA
Middletown, DE
27 September 2022

11311331R00080